These poems have an incredibly beautiful and painful landscape. The body becomes the field splayed open, as does memory, as does love, as does language. The imagery of the body is sensual and electric and you can feel the speaker risking so much as they turn from one line to another.
—Natalie Diaz, judge of the Charlotte Mew Prize

Hilary Brown's *When She Woke She Was an Open Field* are poems written on the surface of the body to be felt in the reverberations of our bones. They are necessary poems written in these times to remind us of our humanity. This is the perilous work of poetry. They are not easy to read and even more difficult to write. These are poems of unflinching bravery, full of complications and difficult truths.
—Truong Tran

"Remember your landmarks," writes Hilary Brown, whose poems are at once lyric imperatives and stirring invocations, all of them asking us to reckon with the body of our landscape and vice versa. *When She Woke She Was an Open Field* arrives with a fresh and clear voice that invites its reader to remember they are always already a viewer, a visitor, a voyeur, too. Brown writes the best kind of short poem—careful in its lyricism and reckless with imagistic surprise—& this collection is nothing if not a memorable landmark.
—Meg Day

"Cleave" means both to cut something in half and to hold fast to a body or object we hold dear. Hilary Brown's poems investigate the remade female self after brain surgery: an operation that cleaves her vision of herself and the world, but also allows her to imagine a self more fully cleaved to the world she inhabits, where the tongue becomes a "prickly pear/ blossom open/ for rain," and any anonymous young woman can still "be fearless, full to bursting, free."
—Paisley Rekdal

Hilary Brown is one of those poets who doesn't look away. Who invites you to stare and meets your eyes with her own always steady gaze—even when the world is unsteady, full of loss and all the slow death capitalism has on offer. These poems provide something else, aching bright and sharp. They sing the queer body, the disabled body. They know about not having enough to eat, about country roads, about church and how to live through it. These poems know, most of all, "There's power in there, holding / the discomfort of it close."
—Stephanie Young

When She Woke She Was an Open Field

When She Woke She Was an Open Field

Hilary Brown

HEADMISTRESS PRESS

ISBN-13: 978-0998761060
ISBN-10: 0998761060

Cover photo © 2017 Hilary Brown, "Field near Sugar City, Idaho"
Cover design by Hilary Brown.

Thanks to *Lift Magazine* for publishing "November, Oakland" and
"How Grief Sometimes Loses Course."

PUBLISHER
Headmistress Press
60 Shipview Lane
Sequim, WA 98382
Telephone: 917-428-8312
Email: headmistresspress@gmail.com
Website: headmistresspress.blogspot.com

Contents

Hymn to Myself in Third Grade

Under your breath
you are muttering
be good be good be good
—a prayer
you can't shake off,
leaving bite marks
all around your mouth.

The Body as a Disappearing Act

The limp becomes a permanent thing
and not just the body's retreat
at the exhausted day's end.
The face and limbs grow ragged.
The beginning of a seizure—mouth
loses water, jaw dislocates, muscle
of tongue an uncontrolled laugh.
You can't look at me the same
or just can't look at me. A gift for this:
allowing eyes to wander over, seek
the edges, knowing it hurts to watch.
There's power in there, holding
the discomfort of it close.
The reproach to children: *Don't stare!*
Do. I look back.

Post-Op, Salt Lake City, 2005

I wake and my brain has bloomed
flowers, their wire stems wrapped
with gauze. My body is a garden,
warm in this cold room, fertile
with blood, fed through tunnels
under my skin. Soft swollen
desert tongue.

Prickly pear
blossom open
for rain.

November, Oakland

Trauma lodges
in the gut, throat, jaw, teeth
grinding themselves, eat
experience until it's gone.
Spit it out.

It takes up residence,
digs the foundation in ground
that slips. Landslide and landslide
and landslide. It clings
to that bluff.

Plants itself. Invasive.
Killing other life. Fungus
and spores climbing trees
with rot. Dark mold
that finds its way
in greater darkness.

Pretty birds of grief
eating the essential stuff.
No other animal
can live.

Russian thistle
blocking the roads
in that picturesque way
it has. Still there's no
getting through it.
Just sitting surrounded,
hungry, staring at the sky,
falling in love with all this
loss.

Dead Season

Earth, saffron yellow seared with harvest burning,
meets lowering clouds bruised dull purple.
In spotted light cows nudge bare ground
with aimless mouths. Trees barely now trees
fringe the horizon, mourn lost leaves.

Through windshield glass the scene moves closer, and I pass.

You, while dying, lay in lost sentience,
gaze drifting to painted landscapes
fenced in precise frames, complained
the cows wandered from the picture
and beyond your sight, lost in hospital walls,
antiseptic white.

How Grief Sometimes Loses Course

It intersects at incongruous places, now crosscutting
humor, which has always been what you supposed
a parallel. It brakes and slows and finds itself
ridiculous. There you are, crying on the toilet,
and grief is there, pushing your hair back
out of your eyes, asking you whether your lost one
would like that new holographic lip gloss
or how it feels not to be able to send her the picture
you took of a kestrel, the unexpected soft red
of his breast. Ever sarcastic, ever tender, ever
speaking in your own voice. Your new companion,
marriage indissoluble and only mundane, a partner
to watch during breakfast over a spoonful
of softening cornflakes.

Season of Rot

The scent
of burning
weeds.
The wet
ditch bank.

Eucalyptus

In summer
they douse themselves
like monks. They
ignite and burn fast.

All that I Remember

My brother's thumb
was all scar, his palm
spit and sweat wet.
I held him
by his fat wrist.

Fires burned
through Yellowstone,
turned the sunsets red
The air was dry in our throats.
My mother stood
in the center of the road,
her hand shielding
her eyes, stared
into distance

Jars lined
old gray shelves,
collected dust. Onions
hung in thin stockings.
Fall's harvest.
Winter's sustenance.

Invocation and Benediction

1.

Beloved, teach me
all of god's names.
Teach me how
to say them. Place
them in my mouth.

2.

God's unpronounceable
name sits forever
on your tongue.
It binds your jaw.

New Amaryllis

Split down center
slit, suggestible to
suggestive, blooming
red bloom.

How to Find Yourself in the Northern Hemisphere

Remember your landmarks:
Wasatch range in the east
Oquirrh mountains in the west.

Remember the sun: it is
a constant. Always rising
in the east over the mountains,
always setting in the west
below the mountains.

Remember the temperamental
signs: the moss on the north
of rocks and trees, the ivy
on the south of rocks and trees.

Remember the north star: its loyalty,
always longing to draw you home.

After Rain the Sun

shines gilt and thin,
a memory
gaining strength.

That Winter the Mallards Didn't Fly South

They followed the moving truck
to my new home, gathered in the tree
outside my window. I forgot
to ask how, forgot to wonder
if this was typical behavior, just
watched them and asked *why*
and asked *will they survive the cold.*
They did, sometimes walking
with me when I took the garbage out
or standing by my side while I waited
at the bus stop. Funny things.
I forgot to be afraid, forgot to see them
as omens, just wondered if they
were safe when the storms
blew in, gazed at their dark colors
against the backdrop of gray
snow and gray sky and for once
felt only gratitude.

Farmers Market in March with Shilpa

Homesickness finally slaked.
I only wait for what must be.
And I am pleased. I watch
fat pigeons, sit on pavement,
rest my weight on my
ankles. Here, have
bread, have sight
of me. It is enough
to be barely visible,
not much known, not much
considered. I can laugh, head
back, mouth full of noise. I can
be fearless, full to bursting, free.

Summer Scene

My nephew has dragged a calf carcass
to the edge of the desert where I'm waiting
in the truck bed. The carcass is mostly bone now,
ribcage and spine and disintegrating
connective tissue. I'm on crutches, but we still walk
our solstice maze in the rain and wind
that blows paper plates and plastic cups away.

And all the prickly pears are in bloom
like fat tongues sprouting flowers.
And the hard ground welcomes
the rain. The dust has tamed. I'm washing
my rootbeer-sticky hands in the storm.
Somehow the smell of death got lost
in all this. It's flat and clear
like a picture.

Red in Tooth

In waning winter wolves surround
the coyote's den. She yips and screams,
held at bay by the menace
of their presence, drawn
by the knowledge of her pups
—a pure instinctual thing,
invisible umbilical string
pulled taut.

She collapses with the breaking:
the first pup found and lost
to wolfish claws and jaws.
Then the others,
one by one by one,
til she has only
blood-stained snow
and sorrow.

Church Lady

I don't remember
the woman's name, just
that her pale hair
shone a defiant halo
around her head
and that her husband
killed four horses
when they wandered
onto his land.

Zeus Watches the Fall of Icarus

Even he for a moment stopped,
and, awed, he watched. Even he
considered transforming
to a strong-winged bird
that could catch this boy falling
in a flurry of golden feathers.
He was only himself—lecherous,
selfish, wanton. He was only
a god, preoccupied with the cares
of gods: which of his subjects
was praying, which lacked humility,
which gods watched him
for weaknesses, his many children.
His mind soon wandered. The boy
finished his fall and the god
turned away.

Drive

past the sand dunes.
Drive
past the dry farms
to where roads
are no longer
roads
but suggestions
Night
here is the darkest
night
you have ever seen.
Sit on the hood,
back
touching windshield,
hands

holding
your beloved's
hands,
watching the sky
fade into the northern
lights
while the air is still
cold

with winter
and your breath
is fog
in the air.

Labyrinthine

To turn on oneself again
                and again
                to lose oneself
    in seeking,   the essential
                    just out of reach. Another
                    wall. Another hurdle.

Climb or turn
back.

This could be circling
        the drain. The breathless
                dizziness of it all.

It could be purposeful
        wandering,   seeking without
        seeming to seek. Observing.
                        Overthinking,
                      judging the turns
                until the judgment
                itself is madness.

It could be bliss answering only
                to bliss.

Eulogy

(Lord divvy me up.
Scatter my pieces
to the vultures.
Let them eat
death. Let them
carry it away).

Hymn

Oh evidence oh evidence
oh exit wounds oh pain
oh plain-spoken oh only
what you are oh incapable
of deception oh heartbreak
oh coward oh turning
away oh prayer oh holiness
oh break-in oh unlocked
door oh opportunity
crime oh shelter oh counting
ceiling tile oh let this be the last
oh on your knees oh find
a way to stop oh cry oh
disbelief oh I'm sorry
oh that blow to the gut
oh skin under fingernails
oh epithelial cells oh
survive oh survive oh
survive oh heartbeat oh
pulse oh pulse oh pulse

Revenge Fantasy

Nothing is as futile as forgiveness.
You might as well gorge yourself
on air. The pop psychologists
and millionaire gurus have got it wrong
and got it wrong again. I'd rather
make you feel useless, helpless,
fucked in the head, questioning everything,
afraid and stuck washing in and out
on tides of misery, your only road left
a dark alley. I can't hand you hell
with its darling puritanisms, but I'll cherish
your fear, your public fall from grace.

Leda

They like to tell my story
as though it is an artful thing
and not a terror. Oh the feathers!
Oh my thighs! Do you picture them,
pale and quivering and helpless?
Do you picture yourself
the bird or in my body?
Is that why you read it
again and again?
Is that why you
write it? All
these details?
so you can be
there, feel it?

Minimal

The guy on the TV is feeling so zen.
Tiny house, tiny stove, tiny shower and bed.
He shows off his one cupboard of food.
Organic. Locally sourced. His tasteful
one fork, one knife, one spoon. He's never
lived for a winter on canned food and milk
flakes bought cheap and in bulk so
there's got to be room.

5 Poems on Teeth

1.
Kind teeth
holding in them the ache
of air preparing for storm.

2.
Teeth my sister and I
found in our mother's
jewelry. Rootless, young,
terrifying. We buried them.
Evidence.

3.
Four teeth the dentist pulled
as soon as they grew in. Invaders,
their roots a misery.

4.
Chipped with helplessness,
too sharp and always catching
my tongue.

5.
Teeth, my animal.
Chew cud.
Tear meat.
Eat.

The Slow Deaths We Refuse to Call Murder

The broken-hearted mothers and the turned-
to turning-away motherland that will not
extend its care so far to save the sick.
The starving. The track-marked arms.
The crowded free clinic with its week
-to-week lottery. The bare gums.
The needle exchange. The housing crisis.
The voice on the phone desperate. *There's
nothing we can do for you.* The tent city
under the overpass. The vote that won't
expand Medicaid. Closed homeless
shelters. Free Greyhound tickets out
of town. *Not in my backyard.* The body
in the drainage pipe by the Jordan River.
A night in jail warm and fed.
Chain smoking to suppress appetite.
Taxation is theft. School lunch.
There's no such thing as a free lunch.
Neglect. Donations that spike
at Christmas and fall in summer.
Lice and bedbugs. Not enough beds.
Soup kitchen volunteers. Locked
bathroom doors. Smelling
like piss. *Pull yourself up by your
bootstraps.* Not having boots. Frostbitten
toes. Frostbitten fingers. Death by
gas heater. Meth and fentanyl. *Charity
never faileth.* Charity failing.
The blame we have aimed
at our victims again and again.

God

is a   slow   large   dog

rising

from his place
near the fire

protector   of   hearth

dangerous untamed

only as good as his master.

Fugue State

I think of Bach
or Pachelbel
playing steadily
in my father's head.
Repeating
the same sad notes;
the coda.

When She Woke She Was an Open Field

The fences had fallen. Words
were a flood. Her voice
was not her own. The nurses shone
light into her eye to mark each hour.
Clocks and charts and signs.
The earth shifted and did not
stop shifting, became water,
became mutable. Memory was stone,
was rubble, was a searchlight,
was a cathedral.

Headmistress Press Books

Made in the USA
San Bernardino, CA
17 February 2019